Remarks on Time

Remarks on Time

DAVINA ALLISON

RESOURCE *Publications* · Eugene, Oregon

REMARKS ON TIME

Resource Publications
An Imprint of Wipf and Stock Publishers
199 W. 8th Ave., Suite 3
Eugene, OR 97401

www.wipfandstock.com

PAPERBACK ISBN: 979-8-3852-4527-7
HARDCOVER ISBN: 979-8-3852-4528-4
EBOOK ISBN: 979-8-3852-4529-1

04/01/25

CONTENTS

Acknowledgments

BERNARD LONERGAN was a Jesuit priest, philosopher, and theologian. The following poems were written between 2023 and 2025 while I was reading *Insight* and other works by Lonergan. They are a response to his audacious, brilliant thought, and living.

Many thanks to the editors of the Australian Broadcasting Corporation - Religion and Ethics, The Galway Review, A New Ulster, The High Window, and the Eunoia Review where several of these poems were first published.

I would like to express deep gratitude to Finn, Oliver, Moira, and Genevieve for their intelligent reading of draft poems.

I am particularly indebted to Imelda Williams OSU who shows me the way.

Remarks on Time

You can buy silk
every night

Travel by river.

whatever flowers I find, sometimes violets,
almost blue
in the sun

Remarks on Time (ii)

bitter oranges in pots, wisteria over the arches

in your arms, bolts of silk,
every color

On the lawn a peacock.

Remarks on Time (iii)

The room is dark
where last night you set
a candle

and there was a downpour.

one day you'll bring
a seed pearl
say do you remember

the rain-soaked garden.

Remarks on Time (iv)

At your desk, your check shirt partly done up after a shower
the smell of lemon soap
Making notes
love I sat under the oak, watched people pass.

I am asleep in the early morning hours
the last of the gardenias

Remarks on Time (v)

you buy a spool of thread
from a lace seller
who has fine cottons

Remarks on Time (vi)

I didn't want to wake you

the rain woke me

he hands me seeds
wrapped in brown paper, from the marigolds I grow

You had a rose in your hair.
Gardening gloves in one hand

you asked me if I had seen
the rose
in the aviary,

border of leaves.

Inquiring

marigolds in your hands

You show me our bedroom
brass lamps,

a painting of the river where,
early morning, I'd find shells,

of the aviary
where
you used to go before the gates closed,
write to me,
each time,
enclose an orange seed
write, love,
for our garden.

A Transcendence of Humanism

you will have quiet,
fresh flowers.

On the wall a painting of

the desert
where I saw rain

light blue water hyacinth.

Philosophic Form

the window open so I can hear the river
the box
of seedlings
Geraniums,

I'll plant tomorrow

After Vespers

the night I left, there were birds on the lawn

you were
at your writing desk
where lilies in
a milk glass
vase were starting to wilt.

a priori

We could see
flower sellers setting out
cut roses,

freshly-watered,
through our window

which was painted blue.

The Answer

All afternoon I read, the notion of belief
outside you pot geraniums

Later
you bring me coffee
A length of silk to line a sleeve with.

Early Rain

a marigold
so I remember
the desert,

ripe mulberries

A Painting to Hang of the Sea

You come in from
the garden
where you've been watering
seedlings

Say, love.

Knowing

the pillow has a lace edge

I bought it last Sunday
at the market from a seller

who had baskets of cloth, lacework

I was walking back from the river
where birds
were wading,
it had rained all night

It's hand-made.

The Letter Smells of Myrrh and Cigarettes

It's raining, late

Stay with me for a while

last night, I embellished silk
picked a rose
to scent water.

With a Violet

a glass jar with a few wildflowers
Where, at night,
you work amber

the curtain open.

winter here

You trace the embroidered edge of my sleeve

Soon the roses will be out

a still life, migrating
waterbirds that come for winter

Notes on a Birdbath

when you can't sleep
remember the night it rained

while I was waiting for you
outside the library
The garden gate was still open.

Garden Scene, Aviary

a bird calls

one of the gardeners turns soil, waters
a bud breaks open

Along Philosophic Lines

the aviary before midnight,

when I bought honey, an orange to quarter

here in the quiet room
where I've folded
down the bed
made up in cotton.

Bird Fragment

He stood out on the sand flat, smoking.
We need beauty, he said.

I'll paint
the heron

where you've planted orchards,

channelled water
feel the fine brush in my hand.

He flicked ash into tide water.

An Idea

Close the window

against the rain
On the sill
where I dry
seeds

driftwood
which I found
after a flood
when I was a child, lived by a river.

The Aesthetic Pattern
of Experience

Myrrh in the incense burner with a bird among flowers
I read your letter

tiles with blue and white motifs

He was standing near the window
which has green shutters and looks over the harbor
where fishermen
work by lamps.

The Image

a vase
painted green with birds on it,

inlay of pearl
You arrange violets

I found them
near the tap

after pruning roses.

Insight, Footnote

The rain was in his hair.

He wrote.

I wanted you
to have
oranges, irrigated by runoff
for your dish
where brushwork makes
a bird,

blue on the rim.

II

Late Quartets on the record player.

You lean forward
violets catch in your sleeve,

say the river's dry again.

I keep water.

Note, 1934

the orange trees flowered
you told me

how you watered them
from a basin that settles rain.

An afternoon storm.

a moth in the light.

Winter Ground, 1965

He gave me a wood violet, said
they grow abundantly near water.

Lit a cigarette,

at night, I
thread shells
catalogue them

while outside
fishermen
weight nets.

Insight, Sunday

Light through the curtains

I read your notes
on being,

And you, love, it's late at night after lectures

You've walked
down the steps through the orange garden

watch fishermen
tie mooring ropes.

The Philosopher's House, Late at Night

I sheltered once in a cistern
rain diverted
from the hills

It was covered in jasmine.

Jasmine grows wild here

On Order (a Porcelain Jug)

in the aviary
blackbirds in cages,

the walls painted in birds, at a fountain

I'd put on Bach,
maybe a sonata.

The only other sound the rain.

it was building up a theory
of knowledge

oranges on the table
where they'll get the light.

We'll stop to see if the jasmine's out, any moths
on the flowers
their wings

on a jar
for perfume.

Analytic Principle

do you remember
when we found the shell

The water was cold
The boat lamp lit.

Pursuit of Beauty

Shells, freshwater, some are mother of pearl

a painting of a moth near
a water lily,

one morning

Begin from Metaphysics

jasmine
along the balcony

moths would come to the windowpane
while I was writing

mint grew under the water tap

a sketch of a bird
between the pages
lavender
that you cut back
behind the shed,
brought inside

Notes you've written to me over the years

Do you remember
when I waited for you outside the library
we walked home in the rain

I've put roses by your side of the bed, it might rain tonight.

Moths at the Oleander

be my love
we'll go to the low hills

where a channel
cut through rock brings water.

Insight, for my Lover

you set the table,
white porcelain,

Open the window, so the birds wake me.

This Order

violets near the water tank
where there's shade,

mid-day, the sun

when they flower, I'll put them
in water

when I was washing
my hands
under the tap
I noticed

our violets are out.

Fine Detail of a Bird's Wing

The marigold seeds are almost dry, ready to plant

I look up from where I am reading

love,
I knew there would be a lemon tree
we'd keep lemons
on the porcelain plate
we bought
the last time
we were at the gallery

to see the still life of a bird on a sill,

sleep with the window open.

www.ingramcontent.com/pod-product-compliance
Lightning Source LLC
Chambersburg PA
CBHW060627030426
42337CB00018B/3240